The Perfume of Pain

The Perfume of Pain

Poems by

Suzanne Underwood Rhodes

© 2024 Suzanne Underwood Rhodes. All rights reserved.
This material may not be reproduced in any form, published,
reprinted, recorded, performed, broadcast,
rewritten, or redistributed without
the explicit permission of Suzanne Underwood Rhodes.
All such actions are strictly prohibited by law.

Cover design by Shay Culligan
Cover art: *Hope with Eyes Full of Tears* (painting, encaustic on panel), copyright ©2024 by Grace Carol Bomer. Reprinted by permission of Grace Carol Bomer. All rights reserved.
Author photo by Michael Drager

ISBN: 978-1-63980-611-9

Kelsay Books
502 South 1040 East, A-119
American Fork, Utah 84003
Kelsaybooks.com

*In memory of my beloved Wayne
and for all who suffer loss*

Acknowledgments

For their valued suggestions for this manuscript, I'm grateful to Kristin Camitta Zimet, the late Larry Richman, Anne Allen, and my friends and fellow members of the Ozark Mountain Poets.

Grateful acknowledgment is made to the editors of the following journals and publications where these poems have appeared, sometimes in slightly altered form:

Cantos: "Old Wizard Oak"
Cave Region Review: "At McDaniel Cemetery"
Christian Century: "Prayer Shawl," "An Indulgence," and "I Visit His Grave on Christmas"
Circling with Poets Laureate: "I Visit His Grave on Christmas"
Crosswinds Poetry Journal: "In the Valley of Goblins, Utah"
Ekstasis: "I Am with the Vine in Early Morning"
Green Mountains Review American Poet Laureate Series: "Snow That Fell All Day," "Interim," "Woman at the Window," "Golden Joinery"
Medicine and Meaning: "The Beloved Leaves Without Goodbye"
Mid/South Anthology: "Transit," "Already"
Mid/South Sonnets Anthology: "Prayer Shawl"
Slant: A Journal of Contemporary Poetry: "Stains," "Woman Sitting with Flowers," "The Rug"
Southern Voices: The Power of Place: "Missing Persons," "Milk from the Moon"

Contents

I.

Transit	15
Interim	16
Snow That Fell All Day	17
In the Valley of Goblins, Utah	18
An Indulgence	19
Woman at the Window	20
Woman Sitting with Flowers	21
Golden Joinery	22
Ruth and Boaz: An Aubade	23
I Am with the Vine in Early Morning	24
By Design	25
The Rug	26
Prayer Shawl	27

II.

Already	31
Grief Group	32
Stains	33
Milk from the Moon	34
"I'll Fly Away"	35
Words Like These	36
Acorns	37
At McDaniel Cemetery	38
I Visit His Grave on Christmas	39
Old Wizard Oak	40
Preserve	41
Missing Persons	42
After a Year	44
Instead	45
Comes and Goes	46
Could It Be?	47
The Beloved Leaves Without Goodbye	48

> "O that thou shouldst give dust a tongue
> To cry to thee . . ."
> —George Herbert

I.

Transit

(for Emily)

At the museum of old trains,
the ever-rusting graveyard bound
by a living stream and a heavy
humid drapery of weeds hung from pines,
you in slim black mourning dress and boots
pick your way among the rubble
of metal bones and tracks, then stop to pose
on the fourth step of a wooden stairs
disjoined from what it belonged to,
and turn your head this way and that,
spilling sunlit hair down one shoulder
then the other.

Interim

My grandson swims in a brief scoop of sea
clear as the sky as he snorkels about untouched
by large forces in his pool of little fish.
His mother happily snaps pictures of the scene
while I'm gathering words for a poem I think
will be about the span before the tide reclaims
its waters split by a momentary shore

like the day a doe hid her newborn fawn
in a gulley in my lawn, then nimbled off,
taking the hours with her. The fawn stayed put,
its spots innocent white.

I watched from my window as night came on
with rain, and the rain turned wild, full of storm and wrath,
and the gulley gushed with it, pushed the fawn away
wobbling into the dark. I prayed, ashamed to believe in nothing
but death, feeling the sorrow of the long night
and the lost child, but mostly the sorrow of losing God.

Then ascent of first light, the starry spots, the mother.

Snow That Fell All Day

Tonight, home from the writer's retreat and warm in bed,
I say the light filling our room couldn't be the neighbors'
as you suggest—they're gone, the boy, his mother,
and his dog, but we both know memory's a magician
and logic its vanishing coin.

No, it's the snow, snow that fell all day, generously,
a poem of snow, like manna to sate what's been starving inside,
like the dog I loved and dream of in a constant dream
where I forget all about her and find her dying in the basement
without water or food. But in this light, I believe she's okay.

Tonight, listening to my life in the cocoon of you and me
and the heaven-cast light, my drifting image is the small blonde
   boy
who couldn't speak with sense, but who, in the days he lived here,
dragged fallen branches too big for him and built an enormous
poem of wood in the yard behind ours, left to the house
   and the snow.

In the Valley of Goblins, Utah

"You are ready now to listen to the god."
—Creon to Oedipus

This is where I meet what I have done,
with tears in the bone-dry gulch.
Misshapen pieces of my heart lie everywhere
as if strewn by giants in the far,
unattainable towers.

What scorching in the valley! The rocks burn red
from the sun's fire and stand discrete,
like souls isolated by pain, a prison of gargoyles
mute and blind, bleeding their terrible
deep shadows.

You who left me grow small and smaller,
disappearing among bodies strange
and familiar, animal and human, all rounded
without rage, for the constant wind
has done its work, like grace abrading guilt
or you returning to climb back up with me.

An Indulgence

> "It is impossible that the son of these tears should perish."
> —St. Monica, mother of Augustine of Hippo

I use the wide knife blade
as he taught me to crush the garlic clove

and toss it in with vegetables and olive oil
letting my hands feel their skins and shapes

and slickness, the same hands that bathed
and oiled him when he was too small to stand,

as I bathe him now with tears in his fall
an ocean away and can't command them, running

stupidly into my bowl of squash and onions,
for tears are not of this world, nor do they heed

a mother's will to set things right, like setting the table
or making a grocery list, or saying, "Don't look back."

The past cruelly presses on us all,
but just now, at my granite counter,

let me savor the pungence
of one crushed clove.

Woman at the Window

Where is my Owl,
my lamenter, night keeper?
I listen for you in the hourless dark.
You remind me of fog, a shroud,
a blank heaven. You bear on your wings
the weather of many hearts
but mine tonight is the saddest.

There are those who all my life
have tried to reason it out of me,
this otherwise sight, and yes,
it is heavy, heavy as snow
on branches, snow in the bones.
I need a Comforter tonight.
Where is my Owl, my lamenter?

Woman Sitting with Flowers

She would make a fine study
paused in shade among the vendors'
overflowing vegetables and purple dahlias,
fantasia of peaches and streaming sun
and the lonely banjo courting stuffed magenta snakes,
the booth of children with painted cheeks,
but one not there.

Unseeing the colors
she sits in a place so empty
only an artist would find her among the flowers.

Golden Joinery

Her fingers lightly lift the shards one by one,
a blue sky he broke, the man with no bounds,
then she takes the fine sable brush and dips it in lacquer
to mend the hurt edges, dusting it all in gold that brings to mind
pollen on butterfly wings or maybe pollen from the Plain
of High Heaven where she wishes to be.

The bowl, reborn, has dried and easily shines to the rub
of her soft cloth. The golden veins she limned gleam
and crisscross like veins on the back of her hands.
How they shook when she served morning rice
to his foul spirit! But this bowl will not slave again.
Royal, moved to safety, it holds great wealth of soul.

Ruth and Boaz: An Aubade

Zechariah 14:20

What is this glory in the folds of my linen,
in the grain of my bread bowl since I married?

In the chill light of morning,
after love and coriander cakes,
a parting kiss to send him off
to his fields of barley,

I watch as shadows fall from his shoulders
in the climbing sun, and savor the tang
of cinnamon and myrrh
still rising from our jubilant bed.

It fills the whole house! It keeps his face near,
the fatherly creases and wiry eyebrows—
already I miss them, miss his body the river
that carried me far, a furious current

pushing me past a hill and a crimson sky,
so far over the ridge, I could hear
the horses' bells singing, *Holy, holy,*
and a voice calling, *Come,*
taste better than wine,

and I would almost come now,
leave the ecstatic linens,
but Obed my lamb is crying,
and the fire in the grate has gone out.

I Am with the Vine in Early Morning

when the grapes are still dark with night,
dew-heavy. Their fragrant aura wakes me
from the gray foreboding that ever follows
me from sleep. To taste them is thrilling:
the round ripe cold sweetens my mouth
like music, the leafy hands coax me in and in,
the tendrils fix me to him who was crushed
in the winepress then burst into the paradox
of perfume and pain, fragrance for the indifferent
hours of day.

By Design

(for a friend letting go)

Cat's claw slips from the fence, its grip losing to fall,
    a green ebbing toward rust in the chill October light
where you lie starved and pale as a dandelion gone
    to ghost. It's true the seasons have their necessary work:
earth spins to humor death into thinking it reigns
    when the spinning is but to waken our longing
for spring with its tricky concealment
    in dormant things enticing us to live.

The Rug

Generations have tramped this rug
with their dust deep in its fibers,
have paced up and down with babies
until dawn's gray light came calling
and some of the babies were cold
and couldn't be warmed, and some
became poets.

Bloodstains expunged from the rug
keep showing up.
I've seen it myself, a haunting,
a vision of men in the family line
marching with feet in rags, marching
in maddening circles of war
who once were children sprawled on the rug,
laughing, wrestling, springing
to their futures like lambs.

I keep watching for the Guest whose feet
must be cracked and caulked in dust
from walking all over the world,
hoping he'll come to our house bearing
everlasting gifts and we would have a party
and dance on the rug where life begins
and wears thin as a shroud
until he comes.

Prayer Shawl

The work of a prayer shawl is to love
the weight it holds, the blue yarns
heavy with the ache of shoulders,
of cold like winter rain, the gray yarns
grave as tears. A voice struggles to rise
from the wool, but the cry fails and falls
and the hurt breast is unconsoled.

But the Galilee ladies who gather on Sundays
to knit their prayers into a woman's fear
and hug her prayers into theirs, know
that in the diamond honeycomb stitch,
or the hurdle and purl ridge stitches,
hope turns and casts on the heart's fibers
and the ladies believe, needles flashing.

II.

Already

Why do I keep looking past the suns, so jubilant
in their rows, to the dying season? To what follows glowing
pinks and daisies bedded in loam, glistening rubies
soaked to the roots and worms turned up pulsing like veins?
Already the blooms loud with bees have folded.

And then to see his face in the window, fresh as morning,
his sturdy working hands angling and fastening,
each movement sure as he levels and trims, steadies
the house as it stands and takes on time ever sinking.
The furnace rages, a sun that never sets.

His eyelids, petals I love to kiss, why ashes?

Grief Group

"He will cover you with his feathers,
and under his wings you will find refuge"
—Psalm 91:4

It's cold in this room, the seats hard
in the church's only available wing
on Wednesday nights, the one for kids.

But it's right for us, the grievers.

Under this wing we can cry like children
and don't have to show our requisite faces,
those we wear in the crowd that expects,

needs us to be fine for their sake, a token
that the sallow horror won't come close
and the dark root we fear

will stay tamped down so we
can go on living.

Who can blame any of us
for clutching the warmth of here?

Stains

You wouldn't think a woman
would miss dabbing stains off the shirt
on a man's chest—
I mean *your* chest, but I said *a* man
to create distance and prevent this rogue burst of tears,
but Lord, I miss that sensuous touch
when I'd sponge his spots of vinegar, dribble
of wine, lipstick, with my little wet rag on his heart.

Milk from the Moon

I can't seem to get past the stage
of hugging your shirt to my chest
like Daisy sobbing over Gatsby's shirts,
only your shirt has no money smell, just
the pure sweet body of you in the blink of time
where I live and you are not.

The ladder you climbed to the secret place
above the trees, the ladder propped against the oak
behind our house, with its wise old leaves
and songs within its branches blown away, away.
And the song from the stars, milk from the moon
gone too with you.

A heaven beyond moon or stars desired you
and owns you with infinite love that makes
my ache for you small as the coffee cup
with the snug-fitting handle your thumb liked,
and raw as my flawed, freckled body missing
the press of flesh that held us in the breach.

"I'll Fly Away"

He named the winds,
the hot southwestern wind
with stinging flies that sent us home,
the northwest wind that thrashed our river birches.

He read clouds like a seer
and feared none. We rushed to the shore
for the scary ones that rocked the sea
that rocked our joy.

He had an eye for bee and battleship,
and patience to wait for gold rinsing the night sky.
His was a technical mind
and his Nikon sang precisely.

He played Scrabble for love of me
and misspelled words I didn't challenge. He scooped
his tiles with a hand immune to the soul of vowels,
but a hand that drew *O's* from my body.

He flew every kind of plane, from Stinson to King Air.
He said the airplane and he were a single skin.
One blue day they sang "I'll Fly Away."
What should I do with his logbooks?

Words Like These

You are stitched into my heart's seams
like Pascal's words of ecstatic vision
sewn into his jacket found after he died,
only you and I weren't vision but flesh
fused for the gift of late years, when passion
melted to honey of patience slow and pure,
you waiting without annoyance for me
to step into the car making us late,
or your hand lingering on my face,
the eyelids, lips, and other skin, knowing me
ever more dearly all those nights forever lost.
You're in ecstasy of heaven now, but God,
these stitches hurt. The wound splits open
with the smell of talc under his sink,
with words like these.

Acorns

LaDeana says it's a mast year and being fall,
the sidewalk's thick with acorns and leaves
that jauntily crunch under my shoes on Old Wire.
I won't pretend I'm unaware how odd it must look,
now that I'm suddenly old—what must those cars think of me
stopping like a child to stoop here, here, and there
all the way down the sidewalk and back pocketing acorns
for the squirrels and chipmunks who run my deck,
the same dearly loved squirrels and chipmunks of childhood,
only now I confess the illusion of being "one of them"
has gotten much worse, and then yesterday at dusk a deer
came rustling through the leaf-thick ground behind the deck
with a broken leg that jutted at a right angle, and I felt it,
the painfully lonesome staggered gait, the grieved
appendage, the words bending wrong from my heart
as they sometimes do, little brown words in my pocket
this mast year of losing you.

At McDaniel Cemetery

I've come to the country cemetery on a cold September day
to lay mums on the still unleveled mound of earth
that weighs you down though you're scarcely there,
a horror happening under the dirt

but instead of fathoming, I attend to
the rough liturgy of a rooster crowing nearby
and the breeze steadily blowing like the Spirit of God.
It's always a pull between dirt and heaven, this boneyard life.

I Visit His Grave on Christmas

and trade mums for a white poinsettia.
The earth has sunk, level now as unleavened bread
of communion, no longer a mound,

that unnatural, risen loaf of the first raw day
he went down, but this ground's recognizable,
a place to plant my feet, let me live my sorrow,
something understood, like the rise and fall
of his body in my arms so lately gone.

But faith asks more, asks me
to leave the known habits of love,
senseless now and impotent:
his boots that do not walk with me.

The recent snow has softened the earth here
and I see tracks where a deer favored
his grave on the way to somewhere.

Old Wizard Oak

His brown, wizened ears stay affixed
to the branches all the way to April.
He hears the icy clatter of the first freeze
that drives the squirrels off to huddle in secret,
and then, when the branches pillow with snow,
he hears not a single bird, nothing but a white hush
and the woman in the house waking the fire
to chase her lonely chill, hears her talking to herself
or an unseen other as she wraps her shawl
over shoulders too small for such weight of loss.
He can even hear her blink away tears,
and he feels for her, would tell her
the crocuses she planted by the tree
are already warming in their corms deep
in the earth, that his brown old ears
will be green, come late spring, and so will the world.
But his voice was given to creatures that go.
His art is listening, to sighs, songs, and cycles of time.
It was said long ago that he who listens
loves most and draws all hearts to his own.

Preserve

Up the hill behind the church to the woods,
the wind rocks the tall pines at the trailhead,
creaks their bones, then loses itself.

Only the tramp of my feet sounds on the dirt path
leading away from the voiceless house
with rooms of my lost love's things still in place.
They hurt, but I can't let go, not yet.
In the woods I'm part of something
besides him, but what?

A gray train of deer following
its ancient path looks my way
and stares at the figure in the strange coat
frozen in place, decides with a flick of tail
she's not a threat, and moves on.

The trail leads to a fairy village
tucked by a child into a great oak's hollow.
I could live there, small in my house,
my small life secured by anchoring roots,
not lonely among crickets and fairies,
but lonely in the world of an absence
no fanciful words can erase.

And then a private graveyard,
most stones crumbling, words
rubbed out by wind, but a legible name
or two, and the word *heave* broken
from heaven, a word to carry home
past trees releasing a clamor of crows.

Missing Persons

The finch's nest sprang up
one secret day in May
in my unguarded wreath.

I dared not disturb it,
a living story
embedded in my heart

whose guidance was,
don't come close,
check the mail some other way.

No one, not me nor you,
(had you been here),
was allowed passage

through the door
with its window letting me
glimpse the play of shadows

and the hatchlings
dimly shifting,
their beaks crying

with hunger going back
to the beginning
of every child's

mother laboring
to nourish the trembling body
under her wings.

After weeks, the finches fledged.
All but one I found
when I took down the wreath,

a sad little rag
whose death was known
by the glare of day

who might, says my heart,
be alive in the air
where you are.

After a Year

The cat makes her lonely,
his sensuous rippling fur
that yields easily
to her distracted stroking,

rain that fails to fall
in the long, parched season,

the invisible Christ,
the detached wafer, O weary
faith without a body.

Instead

I have a cat now instead of him.
I have fur to stroke instead of his skin.
I have an absence to fill and it's something.

Lord, I do not mean to be mournful.
I do not mean to be ungrateful.
He is completely gone. I have

a cat now instead of him,
a cat in his chair, his bathroom sink,
his side of the bed it is not much
my cat with blue eyes. Blue like his
that saw through me and loved me
for all my letdowns. The way You love.

The big cat lets me hold him.
It's something to hold a body,
even a cat's when I can't touch
my love, my God.

Comes and Goes

Night settles in, foggy and chill,
soon to erase the brown sea of leaves
that hung but a sudden two months ago
with such green life, the world felt hopeful.

Now I'm home, have taken off my boots
and socks. My feet brace for the cold floor.
On the way to the lamp, I feel the warm spot
left by the cat, a small, fleeting comfort
in the room where you recede farther
and farther, like words in books
with nothing more to say.

Could It Be?

The earthly dead are deader than a hat,
detached from you or me. They get deader
every day, like things in drawers:
T-shirts or keys, a Social Security card.
Or a portrait on the wall with eyes
you fancied were still following you
as they did when you crossed the room.
Dear soul, those blue eyes are dead.

But the undead, the risen, are free of coins
and grievance. They look with spirit eyes:
flashbacks gone, sight without tears.
The only wounds are Christ's: *Remember Me.*
Could it be when music floats down
and you hear the sea oats strumming
and the ocean's a heaven of stars,
that the poem in your head
is not a whim but a summons?

The Beloved Leaves Without Goodbye

Roses from Susan and a christening
into what I have no idea of.
Blanched and christened. White
polo shirt heavy on the slumped
sacred body. Keys to the kingdom
in his lost pocket. Still
I hold him, pietà, my hymn,
body still warm,
the darling they said dead I said
risen. I said.

About the Author

Suzanne Underwood Rhodes is the Arkansas Poet Laureate, a teacher of poetry, and the author of four poetry collections, including the award-winning *Flying Yellow: New and Selected Poems* (Paraclete Press, 2021); others are *What a Light Thing, This Stone* (Sow's Ear Press, 1999) and two chapbooks, *Weather of the House* (Sow's Ear Press, 1995), and *Hungry Foxes* (Aldrich Press, 2013). She's also published two books of lyrical prose, *Sketches of Home* (1998) and *A Welcome Shore* (2010), both by Canon Press.

She's a Northwest Arkansas Artists 360 Fellow and grant recipient (2023–24), sponsored by the Mid-America Arts Alliance and the Walton Foundation, the founder of the Ozark Mountain Poets, the co-founder of the Appalachian Center for Poets and Writers, and a former artist-in-residence at the Virginia Center for the Creative Arts. Her poems have won many prizes, including two nominations for the Pushcart Prize, first place in the Dr. Lily Peters Memorial Award, first place, Richard Lewis Haiku Award, and others.

A native of New York, Suzanne lives in the mountains of Fayetteville, Arkansas. With an MA in poetry from the Writing Seminars of Johns Hopkins University, she has taught literature and writing at several colleges and universities, and teaches virtual poetry workshops through the Muse Writers Center in Norfolk, Virginia. She brought poetry workshops to formerly incarcerated women living and working in a residential program at the Magdalene Serenity House in Fayetteville and has published their creative writing in a book, *Today There Have Been Lovely Things*. With other local poets, Suzanne visits a memory care center in Fayetteville to offer poetry to Alzheimer's residents. She has an independent writing and editing business, PR Flair.